COUNTRIES

BRAZIL

R.L. Van

Big Buddy Books
An Imprint of Abdo Publishing
abdobooks.com

abdobooks.com

Published by Abdo Publishing, a division of ABDO, PO Box 398166, Minneapolis, Minnesota 55439.
Copyright © 2023 by Abdo Consulting Group, Inc. International copyrights reserved in all countries. No part of this book may be reproduced in any form without written permission from the publisher. Big Buddy Books™ is a trademark and logo of Abdo Publishing.

Printed in the United States of America, North Mankato, Minnesota
102022
012023

Design: Emily O'Malley, Mighty Media, Inc.
Production: Mighty Media, Inc.
Editor: Jessica Rusick
Cover Photograph: marchello74/Shutterstock Images
Interior Photographs: Adriano Aguina/Shutterstock Images, p. 27 (top left); Alf Ribeiro/Shutterstock Images, p. 17; Antonio Salaverry/Shutterstock Images, p. 27 (top right); Celso Pupo/Shutterstock Images, p. 11; Christian Bertrand/Shutterstock Images, p. 23; Erich Sacco/Shutterstock Images, p. 6 (top); filipefrazao/iStockphoto, p. 9; Grafissimo/iStockphoto, p. 6 (bottom); lukulo/iStockphoto, pp. 5 (compass), 7 (compass); Maria Moskvitsova/Shutterstock Images, p. 29 (bottom); Maria Nelasova/Shutterstock Images, p. 25; Mark Schwettmann/Shutterstock Images, p. 28; m2art/Shutterstock Images, p. 7 (map); Pawel Michalowski/Shutterstock Images, p. 19; Phaelnogueira/iStockphoto, p. 13; Pyty/Shutterstock Images, p. 5 (map); R.M. Nunes/Shutterstock Images, p. 26 (left); Roberto Stuckert Filho/Wikimedia Commons, p. 29 (top); Salty View/Shutterstock Images, p. 21; Shutterstock Images, p. 30 (flag); SJ Travel Photo and Video/Shutterstock Images, p. 26 (right); SteveAllenPhoto/iStockphoto, p. 27 (bottom); Vergani Fotografia/Shutterstock Images, p. 30 (currency); worldclassphoto/Shutterstock Images, p. 15; wsfurlan/iStockphoto, p. 6 (middle)
Design Elements: Mighty Media, Inc.
Country population and area figures taken from the CIA World Factbook

Library of Congress Control Number: 2022940519

Publisher's Cataloging-in-Publication Data
Names: Van, R.L., author.
Title: Brazil / by R.L. Van
Description: Minneapolis, Minnesota : Abdo Publishing, 2023 | Series: Countries | Includes online resources and index.
Identifiers: ISBN 9781532199554 (lib. bdg.) | ISBN 9781098274757 (ebook)
Subjects: LCSH: Brazil--Juvenile literature. | South America--Juvenile literature. | Brazil--History--Juvenile literature. | Geography--Juvenile literature.
Classification: DDC 981--dc23

CONTENTS

PASSPORT TO BRAZIL

Brazil is the largest country in South America. It covers about half of the **continent**! More than 213 million people live there.

DID YOU KNOW?

In most parts of Brazil, it is warm all year.

WHERE IS BRAZIL?

Guyana
Suriname
French Guiana
Venezuela
Colombia
Peru
BRAZIL
Bolivia
Atlantic Ocean
Paraguay
Argentina
Uruguay

IMPORTANT CITIES

Brasília is Brazil's **capital** and fourth-largest city. It became the capital in 1960.

São Paulo is the largest city in Brazil and the southern hemisphere. It is a center of business.

Rio de Janeiro is the second-largest city in Brazil. It is known for its beauty and its arts and culture.

BRAZIL

Brasília
Population: 4.2 million

São Paulo
Population: 22.4 million

Rio de Janeiro
Population: 13.6 million

SAY IT

Brasília
bruh-ZIHL-yuh

São Paulo
SOW POW-loh

Rio de Janeiro
REE-oh day zhuh-NEHR-oh

7

BRAZIL IN HISTORY

The first people to live in Brazil were American Indians. In 1500, the Portuguese claimed the land. The settlers enslaved people and forced them to work. In the 1690s and 1700s, diamonds and gold were discovered. People moved to southeastern Brazil to find riches.

Some indigenous people in Brazil still follow traditional ways of life.

9

Brazil became independent from Portugal in 1822. In 1889, Brazil became a **republic**. As times changed, people fought to control the government. Poverty and inequality continue to be major issues in Brazil. But the government has made improvements to help its people.

Brazil celebrates Independence Day on September 7.

AN IMPORTANT SYMBOL

Brazil's flag is green with a yellow diamond and blue circle. The Portuguese words on the flag mean "Order and Progress" in English.

Brazil is a **federal republic**. The country's National Congress makes laws. The president is the head of state and government.

The stars on the blue circle stand for Brazil's 26 states and the capital.

ACROSS THE LAND

Brazil has mountains, coasts, and rain forests. Many rivers flow through the country.

Thousands of animals live in Brazil. These include monkeys, toucans, and piranhas. Brazil's plants include Brazil nut trees, orchids, and even plants that eat bugs!

The Amazon River is Brazil's largest. It flows through the Amazon rain forest.

EARNING A LIVING

Many Brazilian people work in factories. They make cars, food products, and paper. Other people work in the government.

Brazil has many **natural resources**. They include **petroleum**, iron, and tin. Farmers produce soybeans, sugar, and meat.

Brazil produces more coffee than any other country.

LIFE IN BRAZIL

Most Brazilians live in cities. Many live in **slums**. Others live in **rural** areas. Brazilians eat rice and beans, **cassava**, meats, fruits, and more. Coffee is a popular drink.

Brazil is known for its love of soccer. People also like watching car racing and going to the beach.

Maté (*MAH-teh*) is a popular tealike drink in Brazil.

FAMOUS FACES

Marta was born in Dois Riachos, Brazil. Many consider her the best female soccer player of all time. Marta has scored the most World Cup goals of any player. She also works to inspire women and girls to play sports.

DID YOU KNOW?

Brazil has won the Men's World Cup five times. That is more than any other nation!

Marta has been named women's soccer's World Player of the Year six times.

Anitta is a singer from Rio de Janeiro. Fans call her the "Queen of Brazilian Pop." Anitta has recorded songs with many famous artists. She supports the LGBTQ community and works to create diverse, inclusive music videos.

Anitta's given
name is Larissa de
Macedo Machado.

A GREAT COUNTRY

The story of Brazil is important to our world. The people and places of Brazil help make the world a more interesting place.

Iguazú Falls lies on Brazil's border with Argentina.

TOUR BOOK

If you ever visit Brazil, here are some places to go and things to do!

DANCE

Celebrate Carnival in Rio de Janeiro. Dance the samba, which started in Brazil.

EXPLORE

See the plants and animals of the Amazon rain forest on a guided tour.

PROTECT

Visit Projeto Tamar in Praia do Forte to see and learn about endangered sea turtles.

BIKE

Go biking through Ibirapuera Park, the largest park in São Paulo.

CHEER

Catch a soccer game in Rio's Maracanã Stadium, one of the world's largest sports stadiums.

TIMELINE

1500

Pedro Álvares Cabral claimed Brazil for Portugal.

1931

The famous Christ the Redeemer statue overlooking Rio de Janeiro was completed.

1822

Pedro I became Brazil's first emperor.

1964

"The Girl from Ipanema" by Brazilian songwriters Antônio Carlos Jobim and Vinícius de Moraes became a worldwide hit.

2011

Dilma Rousseff became Brazil's first woman president.

2021

Deforestation and forest fires continued to destroy major parts of the Amazon rain forest in Brazil, leading more people to push for change.

2016

Rio de Janeiro hosted the Summer Olympics. It was the first South American city to do so.

BRAZIL
UP CLOSE

Official Name
República Federativa do Brasil (Federative Republic of Brazil)

Flag

Population
217,240,060 (2022 est.)
7th-most-populated country

Total Area
3,287,957 square miles (8,515,770 sq km)
5th-largest country

Official Language
Portuguese

Capital
Brasília

Currency
Real

Form of Government
Federal republic

National Anthem
"Hino Nacional Brasileiro" ("Brazilian National Anthem")

GLOSSARY

capital—a city where government leaders meet.

cassava—a starchy root vegetable. It is also called yuca.

continent—one of Earth's seven main land areas.

federal republic—a form of government in which the people choose the leader. The central government and the individual states share power.

natural resources—useful and valuable supplies from nature.

petroleum—a dark-colored liquid that is used to make fuel, plastics, fertilizers, drugs, and other products.

republic—a government in which the people choose the leader.

rural—of or relating to open land away from towns and cities.

slum—an overcrowded part of a city where poor people live.

ONLINE RESOURCES

Booklinks
NONFICTION NETWORK
FREE! ONLINE NONFICTION RESOURCES

To learn more about Brazil, please visit **abdobooklinks.com** or scan this QR code. These links are routinely monitored and updated to provide the most current information available.

INDEX